DE   '02

Sports

I Can Play Soccer

By Edana Eckart

Children's Press®
A Division of Scholastic Inc.
New York / Toronto / London / Auckland / Sydney
Mexico City / New Delhi / Hong Kong
Danbury, Connecticut

Photo Credits: Cover and all photos by Maura B. McConnell
Contributing Editor: Jennifer Silate
Book Design: Christopher Logan

Library of Congress Cataloging-in-Publication Data

Eckart, Edana.
I can play soccer / by Edana Eckart.
      p. cm. — (Sports)
Includes bibliographical references (p.) and index.
Summary: A simple introduction to soccer, describing the equipment used and how the game is played.
  ISBN 0-516-23969-4 (lib. bdg.) — ISBN 0-516-24031-5 (pbk.)
    1. Soccer—Juvenile literature. [1. Soccer.] I. Title.

GV943.25 .E33 2002
796.334—dc21

                                2001053936

Contents

My name is Carlos.

I am going to play **soccer**.

I put on **shinguards** before I play.

They will keep my **shins** safe.

I wear special shoes called **cleats**.

Cleats have bottoms that keep me from slipping on the grass.

9

I kick the ball with my feet.

I keep the ball away from players on the other team.

I kick the ball softly as I run.

This is called **dribbling**.

Jane is on my team.

I **pass** the ball to her.

We are close to the **goal**.

Jane passes the ball
back to me.

I kick the ball at the goal.

The **goalie** tries to stop the ball from going in.

I made the goal!

Soccer is fun to play.

New Words

cleats (**kleets**) shoes with spikes on the bottom that keep a player from slipping

dribbling (**drib**-uhl-ing) to keep moving the ball with quick, soft kicks

goal (**gohl**) the place where players try to get the ball in order to score a point

goalie (**goh**-lee) the player who tries to keep the ball from entering the goal

pass (**pass**) to give the ball to another player

shinguards (**shin**-gardz) coverings for the shins

shins (**shinz**) the front part of the legs, from the knee to the ankle

soccer (**sok**-ur) a game played on a field, between two teams, using a round ball

To Find Out More

Books
My Soccer Book
by Gail Gibbons
William Morrow & Company

Starting Soccer
by Helen Edom
EDC Publications

Web Site
Soccer Jr.
http://www.soccerjr.com
You can learn soccer skills, read soccer comics, ask soccer questions, and lots more on this site.

Index

About the Author
Edana Eckart has written several children's books. She enjoys bike riding with her family.

Reading Consultants

Kris Flynn, Coordinator, Small School District Literacy, The San Diego County Office of Education

Shelly Forys, Certified Reading Recovery Specialist, W.J. Zahnow Elementary School, Waterloo, IL

Sue McAdams, Former President of the North Texas Reading Council of the IRA, and Early Literacy Consultant, Dallas, TX